INTRODUCING ANIMALS

Animal Homes

MEG RUTHERFORD

SIMON & SCHUSTER

LONDON • SYDNEY • NEW YORK • TOKYO • SINGAPORE • TORONTO

First published in Great Britain in 1990
by Simon & Schuster Young Books

Simon & Schuster Young Books
Simon & Schuster Ltd
Wolsey House, Wolsey Road
Hemel Hempstead, Herts HP2 4SS

Printed and bound in Belgium by
Proost International Book Production

British Library Cataloguing in Publication Data
Rutherford, Meg, *1932 –*
    Animal homes.
    1. Animal behaviour
    I. Title II. Series
    591.52

ISBN 0 7500 0277 8
ISBN 0 7500 0278 6 pbk

Subject Consultant: Andrew Branson
                    British Wildlife Publishing

Contents

Animal ways

Humans are able to live all over the Earth. This is because they can build homes to keep out the weather, and eat all kinds of food. If they don't grow their own food or catch it, they can usually buy some, unless they are too poor, or because some disaster stops them.

Animals have to find the food they eat. They often spend most of their lives looking for it, and trying not to be eaten themselves by other animals. They will probably be eaten anyway, when they are too old or sick to run away.
So life can be very hard work for them. Most grown animals don't have much time to rest or play.

Most of the animals in this book are either meat eaters or
plant eaters. Animals with pointed teeth usually eat animals
who have flat teeth and eat plants. Pointed teeth can tear meat.
Flat or blunt teeth are better for cutting and grinding.
A lion will eat a deer. But a deer could not eat a lion.
And a lion couldn't live on plants.

Every living thing has found the best place and climate
for it to live in, and find its food. If humans destroy that place
the animals often die. They cannot always move on,
as the next place might have only enough food for the animals
that are already there. And they will not always be able to find
the type of food and shelter they need.

Polar bear

Polar bears live where it can be very cold, and ice often covers the sea. They can swim for more than fifty miles without stopping. The toes of their big front paws are slightly webbed. Polar bears paddle with these paws, and steer with their back ones. Their skins are black, and their fur is especially warm because it is made of hollow hairs.

Giant panda

The giant panda needs warm fur, too. Its home is in
some cold, damp, snowy mountains. Many types of bamboo
grow there, sheltered by trees. The panda likes to eat bamboo.
On each front paw it has a little knob to help it hold onto food.
This knob is one of the wrist bones which sticks out,
and has a little fleshy pad on it.

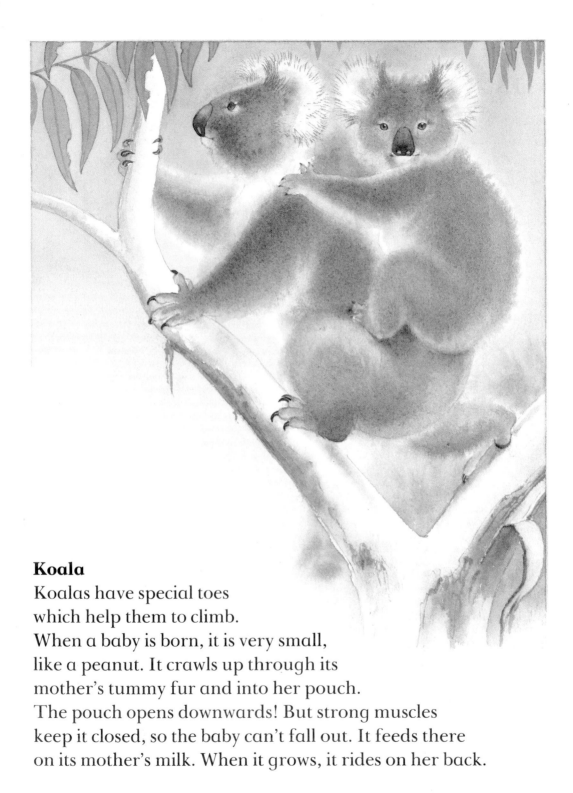

Koala

Koalas have special toes
which help them to climb.
When a baby is born, it is very small,
like a peanut. It crawls up through its
mother's tummy fur and into her pouch.
The pouch opens downwards! But strong muscles
keep it closed, so the baby can't fall out. It feeds there
on its mother's milk. When it grows, it rides on her back.

Sugar glider

The mother sugar glider has a pouch for her babies, too.
But her pouch opens at the top. During the day she might
sleep cuddled up in a leafy nest with lots of other sugar gliders.
She has soft folds of fur between her ankles and wrists.
These stretch out like a kite so that she can glide down
to other trees.

Bats

Bats flap their wings to fly. The wings are made of soft, fine skin.

There are hundreds of types of bat in the world. They eat many different things. Some hunt by day and use their eyes to guide them. Others, like this pipistrelle, hunt at night when they can't see much. So they use special signals, like radar, to find their way about and catch food.

Barn owl

Barn owls see and hear especially well. One ear is higher than the other. This helps them tell where a sound comes from. Owls move their heads in the strangest ways.

Like other birds, owls' feathers grow on their bodies in patterns, not all over. There are tiny hooks, called barbules, on the feathers, which act like zips to keep them firm.

Jacana

This jacana's long toes keep the floating leaves flat
so it can walk on them. It can also swim. The feathers stay dry
because they are waterproofed by an oily liquid when
the bird preens. Jacanas build nests on floating plants.
Sometimes they scoop up their eggs, or their babies,
and carry them under their wings.

Long-tailed tit
Long-tailed tits spend most of the year in groups.
At night they snuggle up together to keep warm,
with their long tails out behind.

Their soft nests are made very carefully.
The tits gather moss, and tie it together with cobweb
and hair, then cover it with lichen. They line the nests
with hundreds and hundreds of warm downy feathers.

Kiwi

Kiwi feathers are narrow and loose, with no barbules
to hold them firm. A kiwi doesn't have tail feathers,
and its wings are small and useless. So it can't fly.
But it runs quite fast, waddling along on its stout little legs.
It usually hides away in holes or hollows during the day,
and comes out at night to eat.

Eurasian badger

Eurasian badgers have underground homes, too,
and usually keep out of sight during the day.
They like to play together and groom each other
before they go to find food.

They gather bedding to keep them warm in their holes.
Then they tuck it under their chins and bring it home,
backwards! Old bedding is often taken out again.

Kangaroo rat

The kangaroo rat has its holes in the hot desert. It stays cool there, away from the sun. It fills underground larders with seeds and other food, carried home in hidden pouches outside its cheeks. These are like little fur-lined pockets alongside its mouth. To warn off other rats, or signal them, it drums its feet. Each rat has its own special rhythm.

Arabian oryx

Arabian oryx live in a desert which can be scorching hot.
Sometimes they find shade under small trees.
But they are still hot.

Oryx know that the soil is cooler a few inches down.
So they scrape out hollows, digging with their hooves,
and lie down in them. These split hooves are
the front two of their four toes.

Yak

Yaks live on the highest mountains of the world.
The bottoms of their hooves are softer than the sides.
So they grip well on the steep slopes and rough ground.

Yaks go up and down the mountains to find food which is not
covered in snow. They grow warm woolly undercoats.
In spring these fall away in big loose lumps.

Alpine marmot
These Alpine marmots have homes in the mountainsides.
If there is danger, they will whistle a warning
and race to safety in their burrows.

To keep warm there they collect bedding.
They cut some grass with their teeth and dry it,
turning it in the sun.

In winter they go inside, and block the entrances with soil.
Then they sleep till spring.

Ring-tailed lemur

Ring-tailed lemurs are forest animals. Their eyes face forwards, like ours. They find food in trees and on the ground. When they walk, their long tails stand up. But when they rest, their tails can be wrapped around their bodies.

Lemurs like to sunbathe. They squat down facing the sun, and hold their arms wide open.

Red-eyed tree frog

This red-eyed tree frog is a night animal. It lives in a tropical rainforest, where huge trees stretch up into the sky, and smaller ones crowd in underneath. The frog can wrap its toes around thin stems. On broader leaves and plants it can hang on with the suction pads on its toes.

Rainforests can be very hot and steamy.

Cheetah

The cheetah hunts in dry, grassy places. It is the fastest animal on land when it is trying to catch its food. But if it misses, it gives up. Its hard, blunt claws push at the ground to make it go faster. The cheetah can't pull in its claws as a cat does, except when it is very young.

Cubs have fluffy fur along their backs.

Giraffe

Giraffes are the tallest animals on land. Their long necks
reach to the tops of trees. (But they only have seven neck bones,
just like us.) It is easier for them to stretch up than down,
because of their very long legs.

A baby giraffe is born while its mother is standing,
so it lands on the ground with a great bump!

Hippopotamus

Hippopotamuses love to loll about all day in pools and rivers.
They feel lighter there, peeking out over the water.
Their nostrils can close for a few minutes underwater.

Their huge teeth are astonishing, but are mostly
used for fighting. Hippos eat plants. When they eat grass,
they crop it with their big broad lips.

Walrus

Walruses close their nostrils under water, too. They spend
a lot of time in the sea, but have to come up to breathe.
Their thick layer of blubber makes them look as if
they don't have many bones.

On land, walruses rock along on their flippers. They can use
their tusks to help. More often they use them as tools,
or for fighting.

Blue Whale

The huge blue whale can be as long as a line of sixty tabby cats!
It can dive deep into the ocean but still has to come up to the
top to breathe the air. It eats tiny animals called krill.
The whale takes a mouthful of sea with the krill.
Its tongue pushes the water back out again through
hairy plates in its mouth called baleen. They hang inside
the whale's top jaw.

Emperor penguin

Emperor penguins live in the coldest place on Earth.

The mother lays her egg on the bare ice. The father pushes it onto his feet and under his tummy where he can keep it warm. He keeps it there until it hatches, while the mother goes to sea to find food. When she comes back the egg is hatched, and both parents rear their baby.

Index

Page numbers in **heavy type** mean a picture